GIVING PEOPLE POEMS

ASIAN POETRY IN TRANSLATION: JAPAN
Editor: Thomas Fitzsimmons

GIVING PEOPLE POEMS

Tanikawa Shuntarō

Translated by

William I. Elliott and Kawamura Kazuo

SARU Press International in association with Katydid Books

Santa Fe • San Francisco • Seattle • Tucson • Tokyo • Taipei
Distributed by University of Hawai'i Press

Jointly published by
SARU PRESS INTERNATIONAL
1169 Market St., Room 138, San Francisco, CA 94103-1521 USA
110 Kinnear Place, Seattle, WA 98119-3729 USA
1150 N. El Dorado, Room 346, Tucson, AZ 85715 USA
Website: www.sarupress.org   Email orders: sarupress@yahoo.com

and KATYDID BOOKS
1 Balsa Road, Santa Fe, NM 87505 USA
Website: www.katydid.com   Email orders: thomfitz@yahoo.com

Distributed in the United States by University of Hawai'i Press
2840 Kolowalu St., Honolulu, HI 96822
Fax: (800) 650-7811
Website: uhpress.hawaii.edu Email orders: uhpbooks@hawaii.edu

Distributed in Japan by Printed Matter Press, Tokyo
Email orders: info@printedmatterpress.com

Distributed in Taiwan by Eric Mader-Lin
5F-7, No. 37, Lane 187
Tunhua South Road, Sec. 1
Taipei 106, Taiwan
Website: www.necessaryprose.com Email orders: inthemargins03@hotmail.com

Distributed with all SARU books by SPD/Small Press Distribution
1341 Seventh Street, Berkeley, CA 94710-1409
Fax: (510) 524-0852 Call toll-free (800) 869-7553
Website: www.spdbooks.org   Email orders: orders@spdbooks.org

Printed in the USA on recycled acid-free paper
First edition, 2005

Library of Congress Control Number: 2005923762
ISBN 0-935086-39-0

TABLE OF CONTENTS

Hunger and Books

There are places filled with people
by the tens of thousands, and not a single book;
and other places filled with as many books
and only one human being.
John said there ought to be a book
which, if read, might turn into food.
But if we are starving we will have eaten before reading it.
If I had a single book
I'd sit on the edge of a cliff
and read it aloud.
What we write and call books
I'll read out to sea and sky.

To the Great Bridge of Seto

My child!
Go with the evening sun where the light is lingering.
The ancient mythic gods still inhabit the islands
that dot the Inland Sea.
You will laugh and weep with them by night
when the universe shows its true contours.

My child!
Go along, listening to the whispering waves.
Unblinking fish hidden behind the rocks
see what people fear to see.
You will swim and sleep with the fish
in the water of dream where time slowly swirls.

My child!
Cross a bridge no one has ever crossed.
As house lights glimmer here and there,
whatever longings rise in you
nothing is more difficult than the bonding of hearts.
Yet you will love and live along with other people.

Giving People Poems

You can't give poems to anyone.
They can't be owned like neckties.
From the moment they're written
they belong to neither you nor me
but to everyone.
However moving your dedication,
however private the memories revealed,
poems cannot be kept from the public eye,
since they are not even the poet's possession.
Poems can belong to anyone—
like the world which belongs to no one
and yet belongs to all.
Poems are a breeze weaving a way between people.
They light up in a lightning flash the face of truth.
Though the poet hides his lover's name
with his technique of an acrostic,
his aspiration always transcends the meaning
and prevents him from imprisoning his poems even in his own book.
Giving people poems
is like giving people air.
If so, I wish it would be the air
that has silently spilled from lovers' lips.
For, in piling up word upon word like this,
we are longing for souls' communion
in which words are not yet words
and yet no longer words.

Cherry Blossoms

Five petals, some thirty-five stamens, an urnlike calyx.
I plucked a blossom in the school yard
and examined it in class with a magnifying glass.
That, I thought in my school days,
is how cherry blossoms are.

Now near sixty, I find I cannot
focus my naked eye on a cherry blossom.
It may not be far-sightedness.
Looked at from a distance
the blossom becomes something strange.

Countless blossoms trailing like mist
is an other-worldly sight.
Though I'm sure no bodies are buried underneath,
the color is close to that of a skull
but as alluring as blood running pale beneath the skin.

"A dab of white cloud beyond the blossoms
and beyond the cloud, deep sky"
are lines I wrote long ago.
A foreign student mistook those blossoms for daffodils,
although my eyes were not directed toward the earth.

Spring

A soft sea breeze blows in from the south
and distant mountains hide behind a curtain.
Although I'm not a man of the soil
and handle only the shapes of characters,
if I lay down my idle pen and close my eyes
I can envision spring.

The time will soon have passed
when men and women use arms and legs, wisdom and power,
and produce their own food and clothing.
We are constantly in a cold sweat grubbing for money,
seeking pleasure instead of joy,
feeling cold isolation instead of anger.

You vanished into Hades long ago.
I'd really like to talk with you—
but what would we talk about?
Here I lie this morning late abed
reading old poems filled with the songs of birds
and they are critical of me.

A Legacy of Silence
(Seeing off Terada Akira, June 20, 1985)

I saw your opened body at night
in a bright autopsy room,
your intestines mere objects on a scale,
your blood bailed out like water from a ship.
I took hold of your still warm ankle
and tried to read the indelible words
hidden in your legacy of silence.

You have defended a shrine of words
that rises above, beyond time.
Year after year you harvested
a field full of bountiful words.
You bathed
in the brilliant sunlight of words.

And now your body has embarked like a dugout canoe
onto the boundless sea of words.
Embodying a silence we cannot impart,
surrounded by a song we cannot hear,
taking aim at meanings we cannot trace,
and sending words to Mother Silence,
you are a messenger.

Trees are Tempters

Trees don't care what others think.
They merely lift their fingers to the sky.
They bloom, scatter their seeds
and, adding an annual growth ring,
long outlive people;
turning bone-white in the distant future,
at long last they wither and die—incredible chaps.
So don't let down your guard.
Their roots, having seized our souls,
will never let them go.

Their young leaves shatter sunlight
and entrance lovers.
Their trunks, indifferent to any tyrant's history,
wear blank faces
and their shadows make pilgrims
in any age dream of paradise.
With their greenness
they invite our eyes to the world beyond
and spreading their great branches
they embrace our noisy future.
With the rustling of their leaves
they whisper to our ears the eternal words of love.

Because they are irresistible tempters
we can only stand in awe of them;
and because they are far nearer to God than we are
we should pray to them.

Mozart

The boy glanced
at that weed
by the road.

He didn't appear specially glad
or even interested,
but since I know quite a lot about plants
I told him its name.
He smiled.
That was all.

That same afternoon
I was listening as he played the piano
and suddenly it came to me
that he had known all about that weed
even before he was born.
He didn't need to know its name.
For at the moment when God created it
he was there.

A roadside weed was blowing in the wind.
and at a single glance
he envisioned the entire world.
Sense and nonsense were meaningless to him.
The weed's mere being there was enough.
That is what he was saying with the piano.

Having finished playing the piano,
he went off to the toilet
singing 'poop poop' to a strange tune.

*

"I'm Mozart!"
he said,
grabbing at my tits.
When I asked him who Mozart is
he said, " I told you. I am!"

Then he tickled the down on my neck
with a middle finger.
I asked him if he loved me
and he said, "Yes, I do."
He said it so easy it sounded untrue,
but I knew it was true.
He meant it at least for the moment, whatever the future.

"Give me a photo", I said
and he replied he'd never had one taken.
When I asked why
he said he hadn't a dime to his name.

We talked on and on
about nothing much
and when he stopped
my heart throbbed.

It must have been three or four years
since I saw him last.
But yesterday, in a coffee shop,
piano music was playing
that I'd never heard before.
There were awfully long pauses between notes,
and then I suddenly remembered
that guy.

I went up to the cashier
and asked the name of the piece.
A woman with a face like a blowfish
told me it was a Mozart sonata.

Empty Hands

Let the glossy black seaweed wait.
Let the know-it-all bamboo sieve wait.
The egg rolling, the water gushing out of the tap
and the gaping clam—let them wait.

Even if the timer is off, no matter.
We won't be late.
Look at your empty hands trembling a little,
sunlight showing through them:

Hands that in your dream last night grasped the briar's thorns,
hands that caressed the soft belly of a lion,
hands that the wind has worn down to white bones,
hands that could have cut off my thing.

Eve's Room

It had to be erect.
It wasn't a desire but an idea.
When the switch was turned on
the middle of the bed undulated
as though a dinosaur crouched within
and you even heard a faint moaning.
It is said that there's a god who created a man out of clay,
but men are not so clever by half.
Stricken with a persistent cramp in his right calf
which would some day turn to dust,
he was trying to create a human being
in a way that God did not.

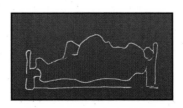

Good Morning

The belly button has time on its hands.
Once birth is complete its duty is over
and it's idle for the rest of its life.
He doesn't envy it,
but he fingers his own navel
while sneaking a look at the woman beside him.
The penis is relatively busy.
It has to labor on
until the woman is pregnant.
He doesn't hate his labor,
but he glances down at his penis
and then gets up with a yell:
"Corelli, a four-and-a-half-minute egg
and a Florida grapefruit!"
He has exactly this for his breakfast
and goes off to his office.
She goes back to bed naked, sprawls on her back
and confronts the nothingness of the universe.

Breakfast Table Duet

Stared at by the sunny-side-up egg, she blushed.
He felt uneasy because the ham was listening.
They were doing what everyone else was doing
but it all seemed like some dreadful secret.

Spiders in the trees outside the window are eating butterflies,
the river in the distant valley is eating its banks,
and one idea in a human heart is eating another.
Eating resembles loving.

Last night, whispering, "I want to devour you!"
she made love to him
so she might one day hatch her egg in this dazzling world.

Postcards

One card curtly refuses a request
and the other is a formal expression of thanks;
these two cards, in Debussy's own hand,
hang in a simple frame on a gallery wall.
(Seventy years ago he sat at his old small secretary
and dipped his nib in an ink well
to write these few lines that had nothing to do with music.)

The script, in sepia ink,
looks so timid as to be almost cowardly,
but in those very letters
we begin to hear a faint melody.
Is that because we are dazzled
by the name of Debussy signed at the end?
They are priced at six million yen.

Having walked down the narrow staircase back to the street,
I saw an illuminated newsflash reporting the arrest of a murderer.
Dark-suited men on their way home
gathered on a sidewalk before a bar among garbage bags.
Though the stars were not visible in the night sky,
the world is filled with infinite harmony
too delicate to be audible.

Easy Listening

In a stone building some 300 years old
in a hall whose ceiling swarmed with painted angels
that music was played and recorded (perhaps for eternity).

But people will sooner or later perish.
Even if I stop regretting it,
my soul will not wander aimlessly in Hades,
because devils will perish with us.

The slender ankles of the duchess that glided so gracefully
to the flowing sarabande are now white bones. . . . . .
Enough of this endless speculation!
Only those longings lurking in an unforgettable melody deserve to
be called 'reality.'
From somewhere—neither hell nor paradise—a voice calls to this
mortal me
in a bright tremolo, almost dying away.

Calves

Because I died two days ago
all my friends have gathered in black.
To my surprise one guy is bawling—the one
whose calls I never returned.
He's arrived in a white Mercedes-Benz.

Though I died two days ago,
the world shows no sign of disappearing.
The priest's cloak shines in winter sunlight.
The neighbor's fifth-grader is fiddling with my PC.
So this is how joss sticks smell!

Since I died two days ago,
today is meaningless.
I therefore perfectly understand non-meaning.
I wish I had caressed more hungrily
the calves of that woman.

An Old Woman

The old woman sits rigidly in her kitchenette
smoking a *hi-lite* cigarette.
"I feel like I'll never die."
She's been a widow for forty-six years,
but is still angry over his affair.
"He may be waiting for me,
but I intend to disappoint him."
Her teenage grandson
snatches the cigarette away and asks,
"How old are you now, Granny?"
With her trembling fingers, she crushes an ant into the table:
"Oh, thirty-five or -six, I suppose,
but, whatever, I don't aim to die."
The curtain at the open window flaps
and shows in the distance Mt. Fuji, blue but barely visible.
Is this this world or another?
This immortal woman's eyes are bright;
wrinkles rut this immortal woman's face.

Hatred on the Bottom of the Swimming Pool

Having lied utterly,
he plunged into the pool.
He submerged in a splash,
and his body became a mollusk.
Holding his breath, he stroked,
and people's voices grew faint.
He forgot his hatred.
"When I become a fossil
on the bottom of a pool,
archaeologists will ignore my feelings
and calibrate my dentition.
They don't care a bit about an individual's deep emotions."
Seized by this emotion, he came up for air, took a big gulp
and let his familiar hatred
take over again.

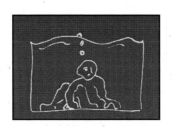

25

Family

"Dad's always like that!"
his mother shrieked.
"No, you're both to blame!"
the daughter said provokingly.
Her father turned and shot back,
"Why don't you hurry up and get married!"
"Well," she said, "you never tell me when my boyfriend calls!"
The invited guests excluded,
the three of them go on talking among themselves.
A nice breeze swept in from across the hills.
Property around here is said to be $3000 a square foot.
After the party, dishes littered the table.
Unaware, the happy little family
stages a drama of happiness.
"If I live to retirement
I'm going to live alone on a desert island."
Though these are worn-out lines,
he actually means it.

The Genius

The genius wears gray corduroy pants and a wrinkled T-shirt,
and walks fairly fast.
A girl, trotting up to him, clings to his arm.
"Great! A genius walking down the street in an ordinary way!"
A true genius, he replies quite frankly, "Yes."
Even walking in a crowd he is alone.
But no one—not even he—knows that.
"That nude drawing you did of me the other day—
My friend wants to buy it for $15,000."
It was drawn just for fun with a Magic Marker on the back of a
leaflet.
But he doesn't disrespect money, because the genius is a genius.
"Sell it for $20,000," he says.
"You're almost an impostor," she almost ecstatically says.
Because the genius is a genius, he doesn't mind being an impostor.
A bead of sweat appears on the top of the genius's nose.
Even on the genius, the summer sun shines relentlessly.
Was the day Mozart was buried, penniless,
completely unlike today?

Dog Shit
(Writing linked verse in Berlin with foreigners)

One was an Austrian,
the other came from Rumania.
Both wrote in German,
all Greek to me.
But rendered into Japanese,
ah! it was poetry after all!
We shared the same impishness, the same sorrow,
the same sky, the same oceans—but different destinies. . . .
When I wrote, "An unexploded bomb is dozing under the fallen
leaves"
neither of them laughed,
but the young Berliners cackled.
They took it for dog shit.
Humans, not God, lurk in the particulars—
here, there, everywhere.

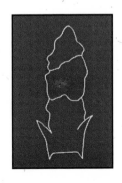

The Old Poet

A rug on his lap, the old poet sits by the window
looking out over the street.
"The way the poplar leaves glisten in sunlight
reminds me of the third line of a sonnet I wrote
when I was nineteen.
The way the grocer's wife smiles
occurs in my fifteenth book of poems
that got some award or other.
That lazy cloud
is my enduring theme."

He reads into everything he sees outside his window
only his own lines of verse,
and reality slips irretrievably
from his mottled hands.

Another Apollo

Now that he's been to the moon,
he is no longer haunted:
he fixes the leaky faucet,
his tears well up in sympathy
when our son is upset.
But he suddenly has stopped
going to church.
On Sundays, he weeds the garden
and reads haiku.

When I'm having my menses
and he embraces me,
I feel a little afraid
because he loves me
so quietly.

Birth

No sooner does his head begin to emerge than the baby asks,
"Dad, how much life insurance do you have?"
Taken aback, I answer, "$250,000."
So then the baby says,
"Then I won't be born after all."
My wife strains and groans,
"But there's a TV in the nursery!"
The baby is silent.
I try to coax him.
"I'll take you to Disneyland!"
He frowns and asks,
"How fast is the world's population growing?"
How should I know?
He starts inching back in.
My wife shouts, "Please! No more morning sickness!"
I quietly threaten him.
"If you don't come out of there I'll smack your ass!"
Finally, he bellows, "Wahhhhh!"

A Clown

A man is drowning in a park pond.
Violently thrashing, he shouts,
"Help! I can't swim!"
I know him from somewhere.
Looks like he's wearing make-up.
A derby floats nearby.
There's something unreal about this.
Some high-school kids lean on the rail of an arched bridge
and actually laugh.
It's a gorgeous spring day.
Further up a red carp surfaces and plunges.
No one should drown so seriously on such a day.
I see no reason at all
why he fell into the pond.
Well, it could well be
that we're the ones being watched—not him.
Oh, my God! He went under!
Well, I'll catch the rest of it next week on TV.

Assassin

Memento mori was once his motto.
"In the absence of desire the world would be formless,"
he said, and picked up the phone.
"I could, if I wanted,
summon the president."
But he merely hung up.
"I wanted money. I wanted women.
I wanted fame. I wanted power.
At eighteen I feared death—just like you."
Outside the window, the silent piling up of snow
is changing the world into a good old black-and-white movie.
"I underestimated.
I pretended that boredom was nothing to be afraid of—
and it wasn't.
It was just boredom."
I plunged my knife deep
into the old man's belly,
not realizing he had long been dead.

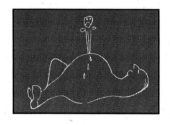

A Ghost
—For H.S.—

A man wearing his usual smile
came walking up the aisle of the jumbo jet.
He wore a blue sailor's cap
and held a scotch and water in a plastic cup.
"I'm somewhere on what looks like a terribly vast field,
filled with light like Fra Angelico's."
He laughed shyly, as if apologizing
for having left us behind.
"Write me a letter with your drawings on it!"
To this impudent request of mine he replied,
"Instead of that,
why don't you join us now?"
The vast sea of clouds below us
was turning pink in the rising sun.
"I still have jet lag
and can't get smoothly into my daughter's dreams."
Then he slipped through a window
and walked away slowly over the ocean of clouds.

A Fictive Hero

"Being the hero of a long novel isn't all that easy",
the guy said, a vodka tonic in hand.
"I even have to watch how I drink."
I dutifully listened to him where we sat
in the corner of a dark bar.
"Yesterday in that bookstore in front of the station
you bought my life."
I had thought fifteen hundred yen a bit steep.
"But in the end she's going to desert me—
on p. 330, 1. 6, in the midst of a downpour.
Say, isn't it sort of cruel and laughable
that you know your own future?"
No ordinary reader could answer a question like that.
When I asked him what he'd do when the novel ended, he said,
"I can die, some day,
in some cobwebby used bookstore."
Then he pulled his coat collar up around his neck
and disappeared into the darkness of the plot.

A Young Girl

"............"
She is too sullen to talk.
"Why don't you say something?"
The sullen mother herself can't stop talking.
The girl's cheeks are fresh apple-red.
Speaking of apples, they can't talk
but they sure are delicious.
"If you don't talk I can't understand you."
Does talking help with understanding?
The reason why the sullen mother is sullen
is that the girl is sullen.
But the reason why the sullen girl is sullen
is not that the mother is sullen.
With no place to go,
the girl keeps on sitting
before the mother who begins to cry
just like a radioactive element with a
half-life of 100,000,000 years.
"..................................."

A Man of Refinement

The dog is pissing in the traditional way—
a leg lifted against a telephone pole.
"All electric wires should be buried underground,"
the man of refinement mumbles, holding the end of the leash.
"Huh!", the dog snorts,
"You mean I shouldn't piss?"
"A city is an expression of culture"—
is this a quotation from someone
or something out of my own intelligence?
The man of refinement jerks the leash.
The dog turns his whole attention
to the scruffy stray bitch across the street.
"What's the meaning of Eros lying hidden in the city?"
Leaving behind his troubled master,
the dog frees himself from the leash and dashes away.
A motorcyclist swerves and falls
and a Mercedes rear-ends a minicar that has slammed on its brakes.
As for the city, it doesn't even frown.

A Classmate

He always came in last in races on Sports Day.
He hadn't even mastered multiplying three-digit figures.
I asked him what he was doing these days, and all he did was
give a silly laugh and say, "Just buying and selling."
When I pressed him further—"Land? Stocks?" he evaded me
and said only, "Oh, trading punches."
My beeper buzzed. I said "Sorry!" and got up.
He tossed me a car key and said,
"Just use my car phone."
I didn't know how
so I lied and quietly used a pay phone.
While I pissed I looked at the crescent moon.
Once I took away his caramels,
and we pantsed him another time.
Coming back to my seat, I found everyone holding their breath.
We found the guy sitting on the tatami, his upper torso bared.
He had a tattoo of a stark-naked woman all over his back.

A Buddhist Priest

"I used to think a lot before deciding on a Buddhist sermon.
Now I don't."
The priest rubbed an ink stick with an accustomed air
and brushed out a large character for 'Nothingness'.
"I'll never be able to match Ryôkan's calligraphy."
Then he quickly filled up five sheets.
He bit into the melon his follower had brought along
and said, as if to nobody,
"Chaplin was filled with worldly desire—
that was all to his credit"
and that flustered the naïve follower.
What in the world am I supposed to pay for this?
Nothingness actually means 'non-existence"
but it's there, right before me.
As he thought about how much to offer, daylight moved away,
and the priest's large, shaven head shone in the setting sun.
He made to get up quickly saying, "Well, where'll we head next?"
and tripped on his robe and fell down.

A Certificate

"I didn't even finish grade-school,"
the old man used to boast.
The public bath he'd worked in from apprentice on up
made a hundred million because of increased land values.

He lived alone in a white apartment building in Machida,
playing golf by day and "Dragon Conquest" by night.
Touring all the public baths in the country in his Audi,
he proudly claimed to be Japan's only critic on public baths.

While making love to a woman forty-two years his junior,
he was hit by a stroke.
Up in heaven he received from a bored god
a graduation certificate fringed in gold.

Ma-Mi-Mu-Mé-Mo Tokyo

What shall I call you?
I know that your forehead is stamped
with the family name covered with the grime of time
and with the first name born out of a warm parental night.
But on the jam-packed morning train
you look nearly anonymous, like a netted sardine.

In a dome resembling a gigantic scab
and in coffee bars wishing to give themselves up to the sea,
you are pining for wealth but already beginning to give it up.
You're trapped in innumerable nets of commerce
and it's the PIN of your cash card alone that protects your solitude.
Poetry? It doesn't concern you.

But ever since you were a school boy you loved word play.
Girls—all except the dullards—liked that about you.
The TV is your room's only window.
Emcees talk to you too familiarly:
"A poet calls our city Ma-Mi-Mu-Mé-Mo Tokyo.
Now, let's find the right kanji (character) for each of these—Ma, Mi,
Mu, Mé, Mo.

Ma would of course be "Devil." Mi is not "Fruit" but "Charm."
"Nothingness" for Mu is too dark. I would have "Dream" instead.
Mé should be "Woman" rather than "Bud". But what about Mo?
You mumble in the lingerings of your dialect and fall silent.
It was drizzling over that pond and algae (Mo) plaited like your dead
mother's hair.
But now you can no longer recall the kanji for Mo (Mourning).

41

A Table Poem
Concerning the Multifaceted Truth
– for the Imaes, March 9, 1985–

Marriage is a pan.
Don't ask what kind.
Might as well call marriage
a broomstick.
I could also flatly call it
a pillow, a wardrobe or a griddle;
but then, these only describe
one aspect of the truth
that marriage is alleviated through things.

Marriage is love.
Don't ask just yet what kind.
Wouldn't be a lie if I said
marriage is not love.
I might knowingly say that
marriage is trust, patience and tolerance;
but those are only
one aspect of the truth
that marriage is a wrestling of emotions.

Marriage is a seal.
What kind I leave you to decide.
Might as well call marriage a piece of paper.
I might frown and pontificate
that marriage is an institution, a system or eternity;
but those only indicate
one aspect of the truth
that marriage is something
we shake on.

Come down to it, marriage is nothing but
a blanket we steal from each other on a narrow bed
between sleeping and waking.
The importance of this is something
we can't quite understand in a year or even ten years,
or maybe even in a lifetime.

And I hasten to add that
the image of a man and woman
eating rice gruel face-to-face
and not succumbing to the black hole
is one vital detail of the mandala
that connects this world to the next.

Congratulations, Maki!

(October 8, 1988)

You were angry and disturbed that summer day,
by the small pond in Miyota,
because I failed again and again to catch a dragonfly.
Did you notice?
I was doing it half on purpose ,
cruelly pretending to be a boy your age.

At a sidewalk café on Champs-Elysées
your father ordered an orange juice.
I don't recall what you had.
You slumped in your chair languidly,
regarding the 20th century with the eye of a fearless child,
and then you suddenly ran down the sidewalk.

Which is really more important—
history or memory?
What a vast future lurks in trivial events
that are apt to be forgotten!
Whereas only useless lessons could be drawn
from a never-to-be-forgotten history.

A crowd mingles in the concert hall lobby.
Turning, you see a white skirt swirl.
The concert is about to begin.
The sound of water endlessly flowing and the silence of the standing
trees. . . .
and you'll hear the faint scent of a flower
about to open in the twilight of the universe.

44

Scene One, Cut One

(In celebration of the wedding of Takahashi Gen'ichiro and Naoko,
June 22, 1985)

"I know how to write novels," G. said.
"I know how to fry eggs," N. said.
They lived happily ever after.

"I have a cousin named Joseph," G. said.
"Joseph who?" N. asked. "Haydn, of course!" G. answered.
They lived happily ever after.

"I wonder if 'being stuffed' is Japanese?" she asked.
"No, 'being stuffed' is a stuffy expression," he said.
"Does 'a stuffed doll' stuff itself or is it stuffed?"
"That kind of question—you should write it down on a sheet of paper
and put it under your pillow when you sleep."
They are munching Roquefort cheese crackers from Delft.
The bar code on the box reads 8-710588000010.
They lived happily ever after.

Then they slept and awoke, ran and kicked.
Then they did this and that, and once fell out of a hammock.
They lived happily ever after.

"Cut!" G. shouted.
"Will this scene be overlapped or cut?" N. asked.
"I don't know until we start editing," G. answered.
They lived happily ever after.

Watching a Cat

When my favorite black cat,
sleeping on a gray sofa,
stretches itself like rubber
with a languid motion,
the tips of her claws
will reach eternity regardless of her will.

That being so,
I think I could consign
her
to Siberian tundra.

Time is never full
in my soul. Yet
at the tips of her whiskers,
time fills up
not waiting for me.

Watching a Cat Again

When I nibble at a woman's nape,
I somehow feel
I'm imitating a cat.

A cat's brain
is filled with non-words.
My brain,
minus words, would be empty.

The woman gets angry
when I say this.

The cat has brought in a bird in its mouth,
and the bird flies all around the room,
staining the plaster walls with blood.
How elegant its fighting,
with neither weapons nor words!

If you want to be on the side of Life,
you should have Death on your side.

Watching a Cat a Third Time

A cat has two
good things,
one of which is undoubtedly
the claws, but

what the other is I don't know.
It might be the pliant, mobile vacancy
framed by her black fur,
or the faint sound of her paws
stepping into my heart.

Before I notice it,
she suddenly disappears,

which is perhaps
her greatest secret,
and realizing that,
I feel helpless.

Being Watched by a Cat

With no aid of astronomy or physics,
the abandoned cat returns home.
How?
No answer.
Only
the fact.

Having peered too far into the distance
for fear of things close by,
man's heart, like the universe, is porous.

Turning away
from a woman's icy stare,
I putter about,
my slippers pitter-patting,

being watched
by the cat
that is lounging on the floor
and just living doing nothing.

Water

In the depths of a stagnating thing
something continues flowing.
On the bottom of a brimming thing
something is about to overflow.

The transparent thing
becomes muddy overnight.
The shapeless and drifting thing
turns into drip . . . drip . . .

Our entire life is reflected
in water scooped up in our hands—
the dazzling and burning
coldness of the water.

A Tree

The top twigs that aspire to the heavens we can see,
but not the hidden roots.
Roots steadily extending,
clutching at this planet
afloat in a vacuum—
these greedy fingers we cannot see.

What is it that roots go on endlessly groping for
in order to stay in one place all their lives,
twisting, twining
in the earth's dark depths
while birds sing in the boughs
and leaves sough in the wind?

Fire

Comes a voice from the depths of darkness,
"Give me fire, give me fire!
Give me fire, for fire is bright".
The same fire that shines on animals' trails
through the shades of the entwining branches
also sears human eyes.

Comes a voice from beneath the ice,
"Give me fire, give me fire!
Give me fire, for fire is warm".
The same fire that restores color
to pale cheeks
also incinerates human bones.

The first match I ever struck,
the brief flash of a sparkler,
a candle wavering in the dimness of a shrine,
the scent of a roasted ginko nut cracking,
the color of boiling blueberry jam,
embers tarrying in a spent bonfire . . . .

Fire is everywhere:
a disposable lighter and the Olympics torch relay,
splinters of wood for the altar fire and napalm,
a furnace and moxibustion . . . .
Fire bakes bread at dawn
and reduces to ashes the baker's hometown at dusk.

Comes a voice out of an ancient cave,
"Give me fire, give me fire!
Give me fire before it goes out!"
The same fire
that illuminates beasts running and crouching on the cave walls
I now hold up between my fingertips.

Light

Allow us to see
and to name things seen.
Allow us—who indulge in shapes and get addicted to colors,
and who try to turn everything into a vision
because of its overwhelming beauty—
allow us to see once more.

Forgive us for having seen—
for having fearlessly exposed the secrets
beyond the limits of the eye.
Forgive us for trying to blind ourselves
by a flash of our own devising,
forgetting to kneel in awe.

Earth

Such pain!
Beaten, gouged out,
torn up, scraped,
the earth has acquired its present face.

Such pain!
"No people remain. We don't need them",
the face says,
having impregnated us with all kinds of feelings,

Such pain!
This admits of no secret whispering.
A hundred million years
now lie behind us and ahead.

70 Lines for Terayama Shûji

1

Big-nosed giant,
you couldn't play a French horn.
But one evening in Paris
you took me out to eat *couscous*.
And you showed me
your dark cracked hand.

2

How many million hiragana and katakana and kanji
did you entomb with that hand
in the squares of your manuscript paper?
Maybe that hand
once spun a top
but never worked a lathe.
Maybe it held your penis
but never a horse's reins.
Maybe it staked money on blackjack
but it never slapped your mother's cheek.

3

You tore and then stitched your mother's photo back together;
stitched and then cut out her face.
Your mother's blank face remained as blank as ever,
and no other face could be found
to fill that empty space.
Your collage
remained incomplete.

4

The tree of words that leafed out gloriously
has not sunk its roots under ground.
The nostalgic accents of your dialect
were cleverly arranged into a well-tempered tune
in your numerous books.
"Throw out your books!" you said.
but, unlike Gide,
you never held a swarthy boy in your arms.

5

Speaking in negatives
is one way of showing respect for you.
You left no children,
no house,
no land,
no medals.
In leaving nothing
you left behind something invisible.

6

The bogeyman in hide-and-seek is ever running around.
in a town where a light snow is wafting.
Where is the 'I' hiding now?
But in the very moment when you were about to
depart from this world
you found
the body of your own, surely not someone else's—
the mortal 'I.'
In the crematorium an unknown woman
tried to steal a bit of your bone.

7

What ever did you cling to?
Your innumerable figures of speech
don't describe the world more aptly
than your own figure shod in tall geta,
a raincoat slung over your shoulder.
Big-nosed giant,
you couldn't drive a VW.
And yet in the front passenger's seat
you never fell asleep.

In Praise of Being Alone

Whether you stand on a snow-capped summit, crouch in tears on a midnight street, chop cabbages in a holiday kitchen, or are absorbed in a pornographic novel as you sit on a plateau in early autumn doesn't concern me. You are either a seven-hued lizard perched on a scorching rock or a stray jellyfish drifting through cold waves. It is our human duty to let you be. If you are unhappy we will entrust your consolation to a puff of breeze. Even if you are happy, no one will blame you for that arrogance. For having torn off your choric mask and unwittingly faced your destiny, and having exposed to air the spiritual wound in your forehead, you have preferred the glory of loneliness. But are you aware that the fleeting moment of that tranquility begins just at the point where the sacrificial cry of agony has vanished? Visions of numerous faces seen through a glass of daiquiri fill the one person you are. At this very moment maybe someone who hates you is also sitting alone before his glass. This is the very person who may make you stand up and invite you out into the street at daybreak. Far from the solitude of an alder and eternally separated from the self-sufficiency of a buzzard, you are a member of *homo sapiens*. The hands that wove the clothing that wraps you now touch your skin. A murmur you alone hear is already in the dictionary. Have you ever counted the things that allow you your solitude? Then, too, you sometimes listen to your own footsteps, walk against the crowd that swarms like a tide of printed type, and try to leave your single fingerprint on the blue sky. And you suckle like a newborn baby on milk that flows out of the world. Your soul and body are severed by a new feeling you cannot name, and you are reborn. You start to live again, cutting your figure clearly in relief among people.

A Wind from Times Past

Lying on the grass, I fumble with the soil.
Leaning against a tree, I look sadly at the hills.
Forgive our human failings.
Water wells up through the rocks
and a wind from times past blows everywhere.

The breath I inhale is a sign of life.
The breath I exhale is a melody of life.
Forgive our human failings.
The earth laughs at my every footstep
and to my groping hands the sky grows mysterious.

My heart is already in darkness
where dreams alone are distinct.
Forgive our human failings.

Books by Tanikawa Shuntarō in English

STILL IN PRINT:
Songs of Nonsense (Seidōsha, 1991)
62 Sonnets & Definitions (Katydid, 1992)
Traveler (Midnight Press, 1995)
Map of Days (Katydid, 1996)
Two Billion Light Years of Solitude (Hokuseido, 1996)
Selected Poems (Carcanet, 1998)
Selected Poems (Persea, 2001)
Minimal (Shichōsha, 2002)
On Love (University of Hawai'i, 2003)
Listening (Kyōbunsha, 2004)
The Naif (Katydid, 2005)
Naked (Tarsier Books: SARU/Katydid, 2005)
Giving People Poems (Tarsier Books: SARU/Katydid, 2005)

OUT OF PRINT:
With Silence My Companion (Prescott Street Press, 1975)
At Midnight in the Kitchen I Just Wanted to Talk to You
(Prescott Street Press, 1980)
Selected Poems (North Point Press, 1983)
Coca-Cola Lessons (Prescott Street Press, 1986)
Floating the River in Melancholy
(Prescott Street Press/Shichōsha, 1988)
Naked (Stone Bridge Press/SARU, 1996)

TANIKAWA SHUNTARŌ was born in 1931 in Tokyo, the son of a philosopher. His first book of poems was published in 1952. In 1953 he joined the influential postwar poetry group *Kai* ("Oar"). In the succeeding decades, he has published over sixty volumes of verse as well as translations of Mother Goose and "Peanuts," earning for him a reputation as one of Japan's most inventive masters of form and language. In 1989, he received the American Book Award for *Floating the River in Melancholy*.

Poet and professor, WILLIAM I. ELLIOTT, born in 1931, has lived and taught in Japan for three decades. Professor and Shelley scholar, KAWAMURA KAZUO cofounded with Elliott the Kanto Poetry Center (1967) and the bilingual poetry journal *Poetry Kanto* (1984). Among their many translations are 15 books by Tanikawa, several of which have won translation prizes in the United States, United Kingdom and Japan.